Alan M. I

Love and Seaweed

Lyonesse Press

St Austell, Cornwall

2002

First published by Lyonesse Press,
Wheal Bull, Foxhole, St. Austell,
Cornwall PL26 7UA

E-mail: alankent@cwcom.net
www.alanmkent.com

ISBN 1 898795 11 8

Printed in Great Britain by SRP, Exeter.

Alan M. Kent was born in St Austell, Cornwall in 1967. He is a prize-winning poet, author and academic. His previous poetry collections include *Grunge*, *Out of the Ordinalia* and *The Hensbarrow Homilies*. In 1998 he received a Doctorate for his work on Cornish and Anglo-Cornish literature. His other works include *The Literature of Cornwall: Continuity, Identity, Difference* and *Pulp Methodism: The Lives and Literature of Silas, Joseph and Salome Hocking*. He has co-edited *Looking at the Mermaid: A Reader in Cornish Literature 900-1900* and *Inside Merlin's Cave: A Cornish Arthurian Reader 1000-2000*, and edited two major collections of Anglo-Cornish poetry.

Contents

For Paul and Michelle.

Love and Seaweed

Lapsus Linguae

There are days, too many days
when to communicate at all,
I have to metamorphosise,
pupate into proud new words.

I'm even at it now, refining:
put'n on. Cut up.
My airs n' graces out and proud.

And Christ knows what comes out?
Some mutant, alien sounds,
learnt so as I could get on
and escape real register.
I slide blind on a lexicon
that's crammed full of bile.

I swear some days,
even the Cornish comes out,
an ancient eruption of magma,
still in there, unrevived,
that sends listeners running scared.

There are now only a few
to whom I can talk broad.
They are orchids, rare flowers,
scented with language.
They are the drinker in *The Radjel*,
the boy who calls Bingo up the road,
the old man sat in St.Agnes
who smiled a *'A'right pard?'* to me
(all as if stepped straight out
of Netherton and Worth).

They are comfortable worn jumpers,
men and women who've not had to alter
vowel, phrase and tone
to live their lives.

That must be good.
No need to even think
about what word you use:
a lingo like it should be magnificent.

Rest of the time,
I'm on a sheet of ice,
huge, unending, glacial,
or maybe some big banana skin,
in every school, college, bank,
hospital, supermarket,
each e-mail, each internet surf,
each phonecall, each text message,
and when I 'lapse back',
when I speak 'un true,
why the hell does it feel
like a slip of the tongue?

Beatun'

Class was a word I didn' knaw,
'til me Uncle took out his shotgun
high on Hensbarrow Downs.
The view from Halvigan
was seamless - all was joined the same.
No split, no crack, no difference.

He polished the barrel with gun oil,
then snapped the chamber tight.
His springer spaniels gyrated round me feet
sniffing the musk of innocence.
Seeing eyes widen, uncle asks,
"Want t'go beatun' do 'ee boy?"
There'd be a tenner fur turning out pheasants
- a fortune then -
crib and tea fur free.

So we drove south, to the coast
away from seamless white on white.
At Caerhays Castle, uncle yanked the handbrake on
and mingled with 4x4s and men
who swore posh and drank sherry in the courtyard.
Uncle adjusted his voice, stopped speakin' broad,
and put his 'h's back in his gob.
They were just dahn for the pre-Christmas shoot.
I said nothing.

Me boots were the wrong colour you.
Black instead of green
- flecks of clay still on 'um
from up Halvigan the day before.
But it didn' stop the boy.
So I gave 'un hell n' banged each tree trunk,
wielded the stick like a Jedi master
and stanked on down through the woods,
parka soaked with sweat.

Uncle behind with gun-dogs drooling for quarry,
all *"Get on boy!"* and *"'Ave us on yew!"* with they -
camo jackets hiding the badge of clay company oilers,
back soon in sheds up Goonvean and Stenalees.

I didn' see the shooting party no more.
Just heard the yelp of birds
whom we disturbed
- flashes of red and gold
that rose from brambles.
Back behind, guns cracked off.
Pheasants fell as broken rainbows.

In the twilight, back at the House,
they hung them up, took a couple into the kitchens
- feathers dull, eyes dim,
birds I'd beat up from the vurze.

Tired as dogs,
in the Hunting Lodge, the clay boys settled in,
next to the grate, t'warm hands, tell yarns.
Next door, them clad in tweed
tucked into pheasant with all the trimmings.
Instead o' that, we got cups of tea and mince pasties
- food (so it seemed) for my kind of scum.
Still, twudn' no good complainun'...

And when an Englishman walked in
(for I knew the difference by now)
with a bottle of malt
"- It being Christmas and all," he said with a roar,
he was greeted like a Lord.

Cups were filled.
Uncle gave me a drop
but joked, *"Dun't tell muther!"*
As if.
I downed the liquid, warm in the December air.
A toast was made to 'un,
but the whisky was bitter, there was a taste of blood.

The toast was from a different class of men -
uncle an' me part of them.

See, that day I'd learnt the way
of men and meat
- pasties, pheasants, the shape of class.

Blood beat, I still stare at the dead pheasants,
hanging through the glass.

Not rocket science...

It doesn’t take rocket science
to take note of our complaint.
It doesn’t take rocket science
to knaw that En-ge-land it ’ent.

No rocket science is needed
to here, fully state our case.
No rocket science is needed
to see the energy of place.

Rocket science? - No, thank you,
to uncover each filthy lie.
Rocket science? - No, thank you,
to know, deep down, the reason why.

No rockets, nor science required
to re-write all the atlases.
No rockets, nor science required
to enlighten all the masses.

Why then, is freedom so hard to gain?
I need no rocket science to answer.
The thrust stains of Cornishness -
cowardly, fearful, silent, vain.

The Cutting of the Cabbage

’Twudn’ no use tellun’ ’un
they’d gone t’seed,
or that the bastard cabbage whites
had knawed the leaves t’kingdom come:
more holes than leaf in places,
a white-green mouldering,
sick, cabbage weather.

From the drawer,
George took a breadknife
and lined up the cut.
The stem, like a chlorophyll dildo,
was hacked in half,
the trachea of it, cleaved clean through.

He held the cabbage heart
high in the air
between Beacon and bal,
like a shrunken head,
a trophy for his people,
blood dripping down his forearm.

It was ritualised,
like the sun and moon depended it,
like village wealth, hope, harvest
relied on this straggly bit o’ green,
an’ the way this bugger cut ’un.

Experience shows.
He shook out the clayey earth
and loped off hanging leaves
like they wuz entrails.
The beast was still lagged though.
He took it in,
’eaved ut in the sink
t’ lebn soak.

His hands were bloody.
He washed them too,
ritually,
Palmolive always, greased upon
forefinger and thumb,
four times back and forth.

An hour later,
he boiled the head.
You never forget how it d'scream.

George bites into 'ut.
Tidn' bad fur last of the summer.
That done, he'll stream the dishes,
'eave the rest t'the birds
who fight fur it
the way he did.

On the wireless,
they talk of the Gorseth,
inventions like *Us Cres?*,
Cornish tartans,
revivals like *Crying the Neck.*
But this meal,
this is real ritual,
acted out, with vigour, with passion,
on a thousand Cornish fields
for a thousand Cornish years.

I go for what George d'know:
cut cabbage boy.

A New St. Day Carol

A day of days, this still, April morning,
and I journey here, past apple blossom,
on to burnt-out cars and large bin lorries,
the rubbish-strewn Downs of United Mines.
This is a pilgrim's path, an ancient way,
from Canterbury to St. Michael's Mount,
so my poet's mind is on Creegbrawse Mine,
Ictis, Joseph of Arimathea.
In my shadow walks the monk named Saint Day,
a Breton boy, follower of Guénolé,
here obligated to set his pure stall,
seeing just as I, the rise of the land,
miracles, and Norden's 'decayde chappell',
the metaphysics of people and place,
a physic dispensed that once made this town
the richest square mile in the world,
a western shanty town of boom and bust,
as if transplanted from Colorado,
set like some tin-plated Avalon
in a swirling sea of slimes, stulls and sumps.
Every third window was a business:
sixty three in 1847,
rows swooping across an adit-pocked tor,
covering a chalice of warm copper,
the ground here hues of cerulean blue,
then elsewhere blood red as the Planet Mars,
where a dark thorn brings a yellow to grass.
They are all out there under the Levels:
Crofthandy, Poldice, Tolcarne, Parc-an-Chy,
Poldory, Ale and Cakes, Wheal Jewell,
and there are streams of shafts, rivers of runs
yearning all the way to Goongumpas Moors,
spirits still there of Bible Christians,
black Wesleyans, bright New Age Travellers:
time's fusion of Pagan and Apostle.
And Ting Tang listens, watches like the saint.
It senses the air move, and when it stops.

Up and down Telegraph Street, Barracks Lane,
names walk here, names as famed as Day himself:
Joe Grenfell, Dick Thomas, Tommy Sleeman,
young Joanna Tiddy, first postmistress,
Jaz Harvey, and Mr. William Wilton -
maker of mathematical instruments.
He gazes from his workshop and surveys
silver bands and tea-treats, the dance, the maids.
Their voices are still heard in Market Square,
coins rattle for potatoes and mackerel.
Old 'Tatey Court' and 'Fish Yard' still stinking.
Walk on up to Mills Street's precision lines
held in perpetuity for the old.
Annears and Rickards wind in sepia
down Scorrier Street and Forth an Eglos.
How they sneered, marvelled, laughed, celebrated
when on this island, set in copper seas,
winning Waterloo gave them a new church.
I stand here in Holy Trinity's shell,
the creamy walls raw, damp, and unplastered,
as if some spalled Glastonbury Abbey.
Giddy, as fairground ride, I spin inside.
It is the bombed Grand Theatre in Warsaw,
Betjeman's 'ecclesiastical fort',
his poetic toy now scat t'lerraps.
but I still admire Hutchins' Gothic,
his moonrocket tower of 'pot' granite.
Now, dilapidation, fallen columns,
a cracked font, neither Bible nor a bench.
Moss grows on slippery altar tiles,
once deftly, lovingly laid by craftsmen.
I imagine your carol sung Saint Day,
by proud voices that lie in your graveyard.
This day, men with strimmers cut back Spring growth,
a buzz and snap that echoes distant,
back and forth again to Quaker's Field,
the grassed over clay pit, now football pitch,
where once St. Day bricks were born and fired,
name-stamped blocks that built this town and this church.
Alarmed, white doves now scatter high above.

They coo bargains, flap an airy fuggan.
These are the birds that will lead me across.
I hear your calming voice, this day, Saint Day,
in this ruin, in this ‘decayde chapell’.
I close my eyes, and in a red instant,
down Levels, I’m sent flailing down Vogue Shute,
at once baptism, crossing, a grail,
the wonder of holly bearing berries.

The hardest thing to do

The hardest thing to do
in the world
is to stand in W.C. Rowes
at the end of a long queue for pasties
watching all the people who've just bought theirs
coming away from the counter
taking their first bite.

Vernaculars

In Cornwall, a friend threw away a boughten pasty:
Twas peppered t'fuck.

The way he said it was beautiful.

In Florida, a cat went where he shouldn't:
I told 'un t'get out ov 'ut.

He looked at me like I came from Mars.

In Kentucky a billboard said:
Gunssavelives.com

I had to ask *sincewhen.net*?

In Illinois, an advert ran:
Earn big bucks! Learn to drive big trucks!

I shall give up as a poet.

Double Cornish

"What 'eve 'ee got next Zack?"

"Double Cornish boy. More flippin' mutations I 'spect!"

Durdathawhy Zack!
"A'right sir."

Dro thebm an leverna, mor pleag...

"Sir, why are we forced to learn Cornish?
Can't us do something like French or German, like they do in
England?
My cousin lives in Plymouth, an' they dun't do any Cornish."

It's in the National Curriculum, I'm afraid Zack, as approved by
Senedh Kernow.

"I know, but it's so BORING sir."
[Ustick the asshole,
Tonkin the tuss,
Bodacious Bodinar.]
"I mean at least Shakespeare has a plot sir,
not like 'Ordinalia'.
It's all God, n' Jesus n' that..."

No, today we're revising Henry Jenner for the mocks.
Turn to page 57 of 'GCSE Cornish'. That's page 57...

[I hate double Cornish
on Thursday afternoon.
The lesson always drags.
I want to be home surfing.]

In a moment, I'll collect
your Terminations homework in.
Be ready to show me
your place-names graph too.

"Sir, I'd rather be in the bottom set,
honest sir.
They just do 1549... an' go on the computers."

Eze quillan gena whye?

'Es.

Eh, sir, if we work this period,
can us do dialect next lesson?

Playground

Last day of term.
Rain - but they still play.
Same shouts and screams from outside.
The playground transformed, momentarily
into an aviary of beautiful birds
- all wonderful in their way.

It is wet.
Puddles across the courtyard.
Drips from a Year 6's eyebrows
fall onto soaked polished-leather shoes.
His feet will squelch down the corridor
and dinner ladies will shout.

It is. As it has always been.
The last splashes of childhood.
The foolish steps forward.

Governments wish to change things.
But this.
Stays the same.

Cycle

Ribbons.
Cut to.

A student shows me her fore-arm.
She has self-harmed.
Hatred and loathing of who, what, where, she is.
She cannot, will not, love herself.

This is no *...Timothy Winters, Lord.*
Amen...
This is hard, jagged hurt,
the bright glowing pain of women and men.

The scabs haven't formed.
The wound is still fresh,
like those on the Christ of Trades
- twelve incisions made by scissor blades:
deliberate snips of skin.
Her young arm is striped,
like her Tigger-coloured mobile.

"You need to see someone about this..."
[Pause]
"No - it's sorted sir..."
[Pause]
"...honest."

She's gone.
Razor sharp.

A Head of Year quotes from the Bible,
but God's a selfish bastard in her eyes.
I know.
I dropped her off once
after a school production.
No-one bothered to pick her up.
I know the view she wakes to:

The filthy Tamar, submarine bays, litter,
needles, broken glass, the odd fist.

I need no silver
to tell her fortune.
I know where she will go,
what she will become.

My crystal ball sees a future client
who will run fat fingers over her scars.
He won't wonder. He'll know.

Meanwhile, she sweats,
gulps air, so as not to puke.

Downstairs, a pair of scissors sees cruel light.
Her daughter pulls open the kitchen drawer.

On my Mother's Bible

I never saw my mother read the Bible,
even though it was always around,
in case of crisis and catastrophe,
like candles and matches for a power cut.

It's a nice edition: *Cum Previlegio*,
hard back, Cambridge University Press,
and *'Appointed to be read in Churches'*.
Perhaps that is why she never picked it up.

I have the book now. It sits on high, top shelf,
right next to my Cornish dictionaries,
as if waiting for complete translation,
black, brooding Testaments, the Old and the New.

Opening it, inside I find her bookmark:
Christ's cross above C.F. Alexander -
his hymn 'There is a green hill far away'.
Did she read it once then, but not mark the spot?

Two, small, corroded paper clips hold it there
to an ancient Christmas card of tin foil,
translucent holly on a silver star.
Rust stains each leaf like the blood on Turin's shroud.

There *is* 'some spotting', as booksellers would say:
on the cover, remains of brown paper,
that shielded it from Stenalees' mist,
the good book's own Talisman against evil.

Next, on page one, an inscription: *Marlene*.
The place: *Treverbyn Church Catechism*.
The award: *A Prize for Good Attendance*.
The date and year: *Christmas 1952*,

scribed by J.E. Beckerlegge, the Parish Priest.
Dear man probably hoped better of her,
she a slip of a thing aged eleven,
but showing up, doesn't always make Belief.

So, this Bible's fifty years old now almost.
I do use it more than her I believe,
to check names and narratives, themes and quotes,
not the way it was intended I am sure.

The title page says that its text got revised,
by His good Majesty's *special command*,
and in the back is mapped tribal Palestine,
and Our Saviour's (now contested) Holy Land.

George V couldn't imagine holy wars,
nor planes flying into Trade Tower floors,
but atheist Marlene foresaw ahead:
Genesis to Revelation can't bring back the dead.

Kites

I

Aow de get on?
I shouted loud, shameless
of both word and world,
as me mate 'Dacky' 'aved
the bugger inta' a westerly
high on Beacon Hill.

'Twudn' just any old kite;
'Twas an "Action Man" *Skyhawk*:
an elaborate yellow fantasy
of vinyl and violence
he'd got fur Chris'mas.
Some present it wuz.

You 'ad t'run like 'ell
through bramble t'launch ut.
Lift never come easy.
We spent dayz on 'un,
aiming for stunts over Carloggas,
all t'Jean-Michel Jarre's 'Oxygene'.

Then came the crashes, tailspins
scattering ponies to dry stone walls.
Is a damaged bad Dacky?
Ess', n' we've lost the plastic missile
deep in the Beacon's bracken.
Scat up then, like the way we grawed old.

II

Most ov us get hold ov ut half ass.
We'm proper hignorant,
an' what we believe comes from t.v..
There, I see kites trail across blue skies:
B-52 bombers, strings held tight
by George Dubya and D.C..

These are their killer kites,
and on websites I can find
cold before-and-after shots,
where cluster bombs hit compounds.
Unreal, like high-speed graphics
off some Playstation screen.

On *Sky* meanwhile, real "Action Men":
S.A.S., Marines and Paratroops
lock and load their weapons,
eagle eyes and gripping hands
ready to rout Ragheads:
Hamerica hagainst Hinfidels!

In Afghanistan, under Taliban law,
kite-flying was banned outright,
too trivial, too joyous, as if it might
divert attention from Allah,
like some kind of nonconformity,
gone mazed, like stray missiles.

III

All of these conditions
are right up there with burkas,
beatings and belief:
women and children shamed
into servitude and submission,
birds with wings cruelly clipped.

When one set of kites has left,
travelling home to mom and junior
back in safe Texas and Tennessee,
I view distant, a boy (once me),
grin, as his kite flies high.
I felt like the very Earth held the strings.

I fly different kites these days,
soaring with words to get that grin.
But kids still tramp Beacon Hill,
and least now, by bombed-out homes
Kabul boys let out string
since the sky's killer kite free.

These spins and turns then friend
are the light frameworks of life
that keep passing overhead,
delicate as time, as De Vinci drawings.
Some of them drop dread, others pull joy.
Toys don't change, but we players do.

On Edward Hicks' 'Peaceable Kingdom'

Quaker Hicks' view of the colony:
all God's creatures in happy harmony.
This ornament under the elm tree's shade
tells us how the United States was made.
A wide-eyed lion, with swishing tail
nuzzles next to cow, in woody dale.
By passive grizzly bear sits lowing ox;
predator sat by prey, the paradox.
A lynx, who looks, in truth, stoned, high on drugs
is, by a pink-skinned cherub, given hugs.
Not scared, lamb and goat graze in leopard's sight,
while wolf's behaviour is most polite.
Just above the beasts, three more cherubs stand.
One feeds an eagle, a dove in her hand.
Another lets a snake across her palm.
In the painted world, all's cool and calm.
I suppose we'd now say there is 'respect',
a commune, a symbiance, near perfect.
Unnatural, though this peaceful kingdom is,
showed too, is William Penn's *Lenape* treatise,
across a waterfall and pallid lake,
where Europeans peace with Indians make.
I have seen the like several times more,
when Jehovah's Witnesses knock the door,
and leave books where pandas frolic with kids,
in a world where souls aren't on the skids.
There too, all is well with beasts and with men,
an ordered pastoral approved by Penn.
Barthes argues all pictures have a prick.
It's where the eyes run to, the painter's trick.
In this, for me, it is the foreground cliff,
as if all might tumble by man's mischief.
And deep under Hicks' pastel blue skies
lurk carnivores, chaos, like white men's lies.

Edward Hicks (1780-1849) was born in Pennsylvania and is a popular American folk artist. 'Peaceable Kingdom' (1830-35) is held at the Fenimore Art Museum, New York.

Steps

"Yep... That Assembly building's mighty big,"
proclaims our driver in his slow drawl.
The huge NASA shed holds a shuttle's rig.
This real Thunderbird makes me feel small.
We travel on, past high Bald Eagle nests,
through a land of water, a land of space,
where retired, a *Saturn* rocket rests,
a steel cylinder in a showcase.

I leap out of Canaveral's tour bus,
like a new Lunar Rover gone wild.
Not for vast *Saturn* do I make a fuss,
but the scaffold I'd viewed as a child.
The wooden steps I had seen on t.v.,
a ball game, from where you'd watch the score,
across a lake there, Launch Sites A and B.
From here, reporters, wives, watched engines roar.

First, I tread in their steps, then sit down square
to view distant, red towers, that poke high,
caterpillared platforms run by software,
that buzz and whirr, to send men past the sky.
I see ghosts: geeky Yanks in stay-press shirts,
black-rimmed spectacles, crew-cut cameramen,
filming rockets, words of waiting experts,
for countdown, steps that start with number ten.

My dad's sceptical of space and sci-fi.
I've a photo of him as a small boy,
and Westerns were his thing, his reason why.
He's sat on granite steps and full of joy.
No doubt he is glad that I have come west.
At home, it was a short walk to the moon,
Tranquillity's Sea easy to conquest.
Jazzy miners flew me to a clay dune.

Pa then, had shiny space dust all the time.
No steps needed to find chunks of moon rock.
I toddle towards him; he helps me climb.
Memories I place tight, in mind's airlock.
Like time, these wooden launch seats stick to me.
Stars, space and steps sweat in Florida's heat.
"Yep," says drive, *"90° comes fur free."*
The bus' air cools both my butt and feet.

Back at the John F. Kennedy Centre,
I step through a neon rocket garden.
Oxygen nozzles grow and re-enter,
and nose cones bloom in total abandon.
Here I can suck space food of dried ice cream,
buy astronauts' signatures, lumps of moon,
realise, through a parabola's dream
how footprints can stay long, and go so soon.

In the centrifuge of me, there's much to view.
I'm imagining Armstrong, his one small step,
stars, galaxies, a life we once thought we knew,
but instead, we are toddling still. *"Yep. Yep. Yep..."*

Reverend

In Eatonville, old hot Orlando,
  beneath benevolent Spanish Moss,
by an alligator lake, adored, sits Reverend.
  We have come past nail parlours, low riders, loud rap,
past grits and gravy, buzzing air conditioners,
  black coffee, that tastes of all the earth, to hear him.

He is dressed smart, ready for us,
  brushing moss off a garden bench, so we may sit.
He has waited a century for us to come.
  When the tape is on,
there is an explosion of narrative.
  Birds, coloured in with rainbows, caw and shriek.

I listen to him.
  No name. Just Reverend. That's all.
Ninety-one years old.
  He has such beautiful eyes,
as if he saw the twinkling world
  the same time as Adam and Eve.

On the trees, lizards dart to Heaven.
  It helps warm their blood.
They know his tone, his grace, his perfection.
  On some history, he's good, sharp as gator bites,
the time he pulled a shotgun on a white boy,
  a hundred dollars a day, picking oranges in the War.

The boss man let him down.
  He had t'sell ladies dresses. How?
"Easy! Y'jus' tell 'em they'd lost some weight..."
  how he found the Lord Jesus Christ,
how he earned some, how he saved some,
  and how he gave some.

On other history he fumbles.
  On Methodism's founder he shakes his head:
"Ah can't remember the fella's name right now..."
  But names don't matter, good works do.
As the basking lizard listening, like the forgotten fella Wesley,
  my heart is strangely warmed.

A Meditation upon John Wesley's Short English Grammar

I, an English teacher by trade,
look over Wesley's 'Short English Grammar',
that he published in 1748.
The *Indicative*, *Imperative* and *Subjunctive* moods
set down like a Gwennap Sermon.
Irregular verb endings gallop in a list
across a landscape of dusty print
tors of piled prepositions,
mines of unearthed dipthongs,
past participles at Trewint.

It says: *"A verb must always be of the same Number and Person with the Noun or Pronoun going before it; as 'I love you', 'Christians love one another'."*

Course, this Oxford boy's take
was all Enlightenment,
on a methodical mission -
tireless concern for the illiterate mining poor,
with God and Grammar by his side.
Even your conjugations bring brimstone Johnny:
"I fear, thou fearest, he feareth.
Fear thou. Fear ye"
as if speakun' broad back Stithians' Chapel
'ud send 'ee straight t' 'Ell.

No wonder Lach-Szyrma, down Newlyn
noticed the Methodists called Cornish 'carnal and wicked'.
They 'ad Wesley's Spelling Bee off proper.
In a lifetime of travel past the Tamar
I wonder how many he thought to correct:
boys n'maids who spoke 'andsome.
Across three centuries, I hear his disgust at
metathesis, reversals, archaisms, words that turned up
like some new species from the Troyance tongue.
An' what of men and women who turned up lookin' wisht?
People in St Ives who'd shawed up t' hear,

first said, *"There woz nothon' to 'un... Nothon t'all.*
We like our beer and wrasslin, we do."
Then, well, 'ee d'turn people maazed
with his words and ways:
"Delight thyself also in the Lord,
and He shall give thee the desires of thine heart."
I believe Wesley dun't belong t'teach grammar.
I knawed it all along. Better if you'd stuck t'preachin'.
Leastways, y'd get somun' right.

Stroke Ward, Treliske Hospital

Padding silently through disinfectant
half-way to a new world
I followed the nurse into the room where he lay,
lungs rattling like a dying elephant,
impassive, head slumped to the side.

She knelt,
gently smoothed hair back from his temples
on an unresponsive face.

I greeted him.
Cracked a joke.
His deep eyes surveyed me with scant interest
but he felt the warmth of my hands
coming to him on this June day.

It was stuffy in there.
Outside his window rabbits frolicked ceaselessly
cleaning faces with tiny paws
and for an hour
I tried to give him their energy,
but like them
he was behind glass.
An invisible barrier I couldn't reach through.

When the nurse said it was time to go
I turned to watch the rabbits,
fearful of intruding with my pity
on his indifference to her words.

I left him there
half-way to an unknown.

When the nurse opened the window
the rabbits ran away.

Jack

The boy was born back over Camborne town,
in a world of Wheals and hand-me-down.

He worked t'Holmans' fact'ry all his life.
When he'd a bit put by, 'ee took a wife.

Many apprentices went through his hands.
He d'knaw faather and all the brass bands.

'Ee slept each night, untroubled, like a log.
Made tea, crowst, tramped off inta' mornin' fog.

All told see, his world was a small sphere:
all die-cutting, compressors and head gear.

Like many a Cornishman in life's lot,
he was plain satisfied with what 'ee got.

What Lord God sent, was good enough fur they.
"Naw, I dun't want fur nothun'," he would say.

When missus passed on, he went pub more weeks
and bristle-kissed sweet, young maids on their cheeks.

Then, when time got tricky, and cancer spread,
there was, in Jack, no fear, no hint of dread.

In St. Hilary church, a wooden box,
where Jack, eventually, Death did coax.

Annie Walke's bright angels would take 'un on.
A quick hymn, a few tears, and he was gone.

Lines for Laity (An elegy for Paul Laity 1928-2001)

I think of you Paul, this last day of summer,
when the grass is cut, when the hay is mown.
This is a time you'd be at your allotment.

"Do you like gardening?" you asked me.
"Yes," I said, though knowing
it could never be the way you liked it
- as if you knew.

Your name ('Dairy' in the old tongue),
winds down to me like a stubborn bull
stuck in a granite-walled bowgie.
I think of you that way Paul:
strong, solid, waiting.

I think of you Paul, in collar and tie
at Tim and Ceri's wedding,
unashamed, us taking other tables' unused wine.
You and I grizzling up at Tim's speech.

You see the aim, for you strove hard.
You were on the side of right, then, now, forever.

I hear you Paul
in those days when we read Sir George Harrison,
when we spoke of Brian Hambley,
when we shaped book of books,
revolution plotted upon a lap-top,
and you defying all.

Me awe-struck, while cats watched through the porch window,
and pawed at us for warmth, for affection.
At times you asked if I need another *Guinness*.
"No," I said, but still you poured it.

Joan would ask you to lay the table,
and calling her 'darling', so gently,

so lovingly,
as if in Shakespeare,
you placed books down
and began to set the places.

You went too soon Paul.
You took too much with you
that day.

Part of Stannary,
part of independence,
part of freedom died.
And part of me died too.

Back in June, I see the baking-hot committal,
black voices, full summer,
drowned out by Bristol airport's jets:
a vicar mouthing useless words.

I prefer other words:
the times we talked of poetry, of Rowse,
of John Willie Thomas, Methodist Preacher in St Just,
and *"the wickedness of the last days,*
the poor illiterate miner who never knew the word of God",
of your defences, your trials,
the Navy, Falmouth,
Cornwall then, and Cornwall now.
What long laughs we had,
what short days we spent.

Paul, the best compliment of all:
you didn' ever talk like a lawyer.

I take all that you lived for Paul,
all that you loved.
This side of the grave,
with this pen,
the pen with which I write our book,
I paw at you,
not through the window,

where those cats watched us work,
but across time and space, with this poem,
for warmth, affection,
for Laity, your law, your life.

For Benjamin Luxon, in his sickness

I hope this winter day, you aren't alone.
I feel your confusion baritone,
how tinitus stops your musical dreams,
hard for one who has swum the finest streams.

Irony of ironies I feel,
how life turns on fortune's fickle wheel.
I wonder how hellish it is good friend,
to find this silence your new found stipend.

When Britten wrote you *Owen Wingraves'* role,
of ear, melody, you had such control.
I've seen film of you on every stage,
lifting opera high above the page.

You've ignited passion in the dullest scores,
taken Cornish *canow* to far off shores.
If I, as a Merlin, could magic do,
your hearing's return, I would pursue,

waving wand to bring back sound crystal clear,
to ease your heartache, frustration and fear.
But words are all the comfort I can give.
Read them aloud and let my rhymes live.

Your voice does them better justice than I.
Your language rings across a granite sky.
Your syllables reach the mineshafts of me,
and run joyous to Perranuthnoe's sea.

Take faith in this and your music and song.
To history, legend, you roar headlong.

At Freiburg Münster

Green-black bells toll the way they do,
seemingly as in all European cities,

announcing both rat-carried Black Plague
and Jesus Christ have walked into town.

Their toll drifts as if spring pollen dust
up the post-glacial valleys of the Schwarzwald,

while below traders still sell pretzels and bratwurst.
Old women brush up the snipped stems of flowers.

On red sandstone walls, ancient carvings
give past sizes of bread for barterers,

while parked BMW and cable television companies
now point market browsers to new icons,

but it is in the tower's resonance
that all these times meet.

Not a miracle conversion
but as the truest juxtaposition,

how an echo of the bells can transport even
the lapsed Methodist to his Heaven.

Breton Return

I Paul's Cormorants

I follow in your saintly footsteps Paul,
and cross the long Channel to *Penn-ar-Bed*,
- Brythonic refugee heading to Gaul,
to your bishopric, de Léon I'm led.

Aurelian, from ferry's reclined seat,
I see the shimmering *Île de Batz*,
where a fierce dragon you expelled and beat,
founding your monastery by rocky flats.

On a magical, pink granite outcrop
three cormorants - dragons - with outstretched wings
shriek black, then as prehistoric darts drop
to catch what shoals of fish the blue tide brings.

Phalacrocorax, St. Paul saw you too,
when in days dark, his coracle hit coast.
Their long necks swivelled, to geek, and him view.
God's creatures / nature's gargoyles, his host.

Inland, by the high *Kreisker* bell tower
lies his cathedral, its twin spires tall
above far fields of cauliflower.
Here I meet tangible ghosts of Cornwall.

With shiny Euros I purchase a guide
and wander through Truro's Breton design.
There, sallow, rising Norman columns hide
the Host, reliquary, shrine upon shrine.

Outside, artics carrying artichokes
rumble refrigerated past you Pol,
a sound and symmetry that high up, stokes
the *Pardon* day's tower-bell and its toll.

Hearing it, I am back in Paul, Penwith,
at your small church high above Gwavas Lake,
beside Dolly's memorial and myth.
You're holding water, waves, herring and hake,

like some strange Meriasek in reverse,
whose Camborne drama also comes to mind.
Here, time has a habit to intersperse
as transept walls makes history rewind.

St. Paul, you never knew of this or me,
and yet those same colonies I now stank:
Carantec, *Croas-ar-Born* and *Penzé*
are like a sot Cornwall so deeply drank,

a mead recipe already set down
by the Breton monk who in 884
wrote your life from far Wales to this town,
which new chroniclers like me can't ignore.

All centuries and crossings pale though
when down the far left, sunlit-streamed transept
I stand before bright stained glass, shaped just so
by some glazier, naïve, yet adept.

This window matches believers with place.
Centuries of crossings the future face.
Three cormorants light up a Bible scene,
Paul's glossy birds: Celtic, Godly, serene.

II Ode to Moguériec

Moguériec, Moguériec,
where rock and sea are forever set.
Moguériec, Moguériec,
a place, a space that I won't forget.

This April evening I walk your shore
with clocks changed and the day long and hot.
I breath in deep your legend and lore,
thinking of all that's gone, all I've got.

Moguériec, Moguériec,
where rock and sea come to pirouette.
Moguériec, Moguériec,
a place, a space, a still statuette.

Coast of red onions, coast of surf,
I look north to home, both love and hurt.
Some days ache, some offer wondrous worth.
This day is such, so these lines I blurt.

Moguériec, Moguériec,
where rock and sea both foam and sweat.
Moguériec, Moguériec,
a place, a space without one regret.

Odes to places aren't my normal style,
but here I'll dive in, get dripping wet.
Such sun on such stone makes me ductile.
Never have I yearned for sun to set.

Moguériec, Moguériec,
where rock and sea run wild and wet.
Moguériec, Moguériec,
a place, a space where time is tacit.

Stillness, grace, mind's peace are all here.
You instruct me like a tide table,
and future navigations come clear,
as night ends this Breton fable.

Moguériec, Moguériec,
where rock and sea I came and met.
Moguériec, Moguériec,
a place, a place time will not forget.

III Gathering Seaweed, Île de Batz

In the dark deluge that once flooded *Ys*[1]
women, with hands the colour of lichen
delve delicately into the sea's depths
and with deft hooks, pull out the swirling threads,
backs so bent, it is now unnatural
for them to stand and feel the hot sun.
They are tiny white crescents on the strand.
But last night's storm has been kindly to them -
vast seaweed tangles have been left behind,
Atlantic's present for the *Île de Batz.*
The scooping continues in the same way
as their grandmothers and those before them,
always algae to be washed from skirt hems.
In places tractors and trailers trundle,
but on the *Île*, half-submerged horses
pull delicate wagons into the tide.
Beneath, their hooves press deep into the sand
while above, the leaking crop is pitched up.
Men, all smelling of salt, join their partners
twisting their *scoubidou*[2] into the fronds.
There is much love in this work, craft and life
like they are the very last in their line.
The Breton word: *Goëmon*[3] is on their lips,
a word watched, mouthed, sung and told for aeons.
The weed is endless, relentless, but loved.
Limpets get tossed aside, as do small crabs,
who unwanted plop into the deep green.
On shore, on sandy beaches of the isle,
the women carefully unwind the slime,
so it may then dry, and crackle, and pop -
all of the aqua evaporated.
Twice a week the crisp crop is turned over
then pitched high on to primitive barrows.
Women waddle with them across the dunes
dumping the strands into ricks of blackness,
where it is burnt to release its richness.
From brown fields distant, farmers smile,

knowing that the barter will soon be done.
Close up, ancient men, the colour of kelp,
polyped women and extracts of children
make twilight offerings to seaweed gods.
  Meantime, the unfair sea keeps creating,
an unstoppable *Fucus*[4] factory.
It knows all the seaweed's deepest secrets:
brown air sacs that science names vesicles,
hormones, vitamins, elements, proteins
that in Roscoff's Thalassotherapy
makes for trendy cosmetics, soaps, cooking.
  At night the crop ceases in all but dreams.
Women, with hands the colour of lichen,
flail, turn and twist in white linen beds.
Their eyelids flitter in some deep REM sleep,
expectant for golden algae, tin kelp,
hopeful that sometime soon, the flood might cease.

1. In Breton folklore, Ys was a beautiful island city in the Bay of Douarnenez, who the devil flooded.
2. This is a rotating, screw-like tool, used to collect seaweed.
3. Breton: seaweed.
4. The most common kind of seaweed found in Brittany.

IV Tourist Gaze

Always, always, always,
that cross-Channel envy,
like we're not good enough.
Armorican betterment,
the way Jenner loved his Breton.
He was made a bard there in 1901,
not holding out much for enlightened Methodism.
Instead, he preferred calvaries and cults.
The implication: Cornwall fucked up.
Best learn from the Sons of Ermine.

Now we've bookshops named
'Gwynn ha Du' like Morvan Marchal on acid,
imported *fest-noz*, webcasts of circle dances with pinkies,
instruments called *bombardes* and *biniou*,
but Cornwall's no Brittany.
Coiffes are no Gooks, Perranporth's no Lorient,
the Hurlers are no Carnac,
St Michael's Mount's no Mont-St-Michel,
John Harris' *Lays* are no ancient *lais*, KER's no BZH.
You'd be mazed to gaze this way pard.

Annoyed at our incompetence,
betrayal, inferiority complex,
ashamed that we've no convocation,
no pride, no pan-Celticism we won't ride,
I re-read that early tourist to Brittany -
canny Cap'n Harry Carter, smuggler,
precision Methodist, of Prussia Cove,
to hear it like it is, him locked up in old Roscoff.
His gaze, our gaze, his failing, our failing
tickles me tourist ass.

The Tin Tea Set

No silver service, or white porcelain,
  nor bone china, plastic, or earthenware,
but a full dinner service made of tin.
  That's proper, and I s'pect, goodly and rare.

The Cornish call evening dinner 'tea',
  so that is what I will label the set,
once held at Botallack Count House, you see,
  made by the city of Sheffield's sweat.

The set was commissioned in '43
  by Mr. Stephen Harvey James, Agent,
to cause demand and a tin spending-spree.
  But although good, not all things are meant.

The tin tea set never 'zactly took off.
  They all liked their crocks banded blue and white.
Besides, bal pasties scoffed, didn' need no trough.
  Saffron cake tastes better off china bright.

When Prince and Princess visited the mine,
  no doubt the tin tea set sat polished up.
"How frightfully novel!" - the Prince's line,
  as champagne fizzed in a long lost, tin cup.

Protecting Power visits Stannum's core
  to see this mole nation, who clink below
but Tinner's worth falls on an English shore.
  Tin, tea, poverty - it's always been so.

The tea set is now a world away
  from R.M. Ballantyne's *Deep Down* mine tale.
There, Zackey Booy, Maggot, knack n' assay
  where *Sn* was the only true Grail.

When the mine shut, the tin tea set travelled.
  Feared destroyed, it turned up in Florida,
a lost lode by a relative there held:
  fate, heritage, time to reconsider.

Today, *Kneehigh Theatre* walk arsenic flues.
  Long gone is the Cap'n, Prince and Princess.
Come tourists for drama, copper blue views,
  not tin tea sets, nor untidy mine mess.

I've walked these 'An Gof' scrawled ruins enough,
  seen postcards aplenty of the Crowns pair,
and dream of this tea set, ready and rough,
  cakes, clotted cream, a platter full and fair.

Now the tin tea set is housed at Geevor
  in a glass cabinet of history,
between sea and shaft, mundic and the moor.
  Tin and tea, lost in western mystery.

Stations

In the bus station café,
the Down's Syndrome girl scrapes plates.
She smiles, knows her work is important.
The grease must go.

Good they find people like her jobs edn' ut?

Here is the underworld,
the underclass of us,
what we like to brush under the mat,
dregs whom planners, councillors forget.

I seed un on the news las' night.

Outside, on the floor, countless fag ends,
spit, discarded *Special Brew* cans.
It reeks of sweat, vomit, urine,
the rotting pasties that gulls fight over.

'Tis enough t'make 'ee heave.

A woman with a wrinkled,
rouged face, sips a coffee,
draws deep on a *Silk Cut*.
She knows this is as good as it gets.

I seen her here week 'afore last.

Old men who long should
have had hip replacements
know their place, call each other boy,
knowing the order of things.

They gived ut out on the wireless.

Soft milky women whose pierced bellies,
flab out over hipsters bawl at their kids.
They rue the bastarding day
they let men touch them.

You knaw what tis like.

Buses arrive, advertising other roles,
films, models, fantasies,
places this crowd won't ever go.
Instead, they list from station to station.

They changed the time o' that one.

Those who travel from here
are the old, the infirm, the insane,
the poor, the rotting and the dead.
They cast a circle and curse.

Thas' the way tis. 'Es.

Soon, they join diesel fumes,
enter easy access doors,
to wild destinations, exotica:
Shittin' hell: St Ives, via Camborne.

Best bet is to knaw yer place.

Euchre Match

Shuffled lives come together.
Dealt hope reaches skywards,
as they square up like bottles o' piss.
Tonight, live: Probus take on Meva'.
The deck faces old grudges,
hard as rugby, wrasslin', hurlin',
and other shite pastimes we mind.
This hurts. It bruises. It's bloody.
No prisoners boy.

The table's coozen'd off,
and sticky cards are laid down,
next to Hicks' Special Draft, pints of Sharps.
Tricks are quick, for nines upwards.
Right bower, then left.
Eyes silent, mouths still.
Stonewallers run.
Loners for four points.
You sweat like a bull.

Then comes the Benny,
a card that hits, heat-seeking,
guided in, sharp as a tomahawk.
You need Chobham armour to survive,
so pride takes over,
like Trevithick tak'n on an alligator.
To null it, you sup more beer.
You best knaw that this is more than
a matter of clarity, charity, cards.

Me da's a euchre champion.
There are crappy trophies
littering ma's sideboard,
all felt, aces high and imitation silver.
It dun't matter. He's in them.
One day, they'll be mine.

These are the trophies of his wars,
past conflicts, his claywork 'Nams,
his V.C.s. pinned to a swelling chest.

Soft (a poet no less)
and sipping Guinness,
I watch hands cross the table.
Arms slide. Cards flick and turn.
Rivals slobber like new sturts.
Ash drops. Tobacco lingers.
Farts brew deep inside and pass.
For the Cornish, this game hurts.
It hurts as hard as love.

Benny's gone idn' a?

Whims

Stuck in traffic, I watch
a beautiful girl. She makes other driver's stare.
In her hand, she holds a glossy magazine,
filled with romance, make-overs, celebrity weddings,
colour you dun't get in Cornwall.

Carn Brea, old, rising, cynic, frowns on her,
slipping down his December fog,
drowning all ("paparazzi and gossip") in dull granite,
sick stains, rancid gum-chewed pavements that
stick you to a past you dun't wun't.

She is met by her lover. They link.
The whim of me, feels their passion,
the way their lips compress,
saliva eroding surfaces as love lampreys,
while slimed tongues flick for silver.

Tomorrow, their lips will be numb.
Bruised, they wish they hadn't kissed so hard,
There are whelks where they bit like dogs,
chaps where skin hits the cold air,
fusion like neither was gone.

He is virulent, raising ore,
like no whim could ever,
would ever, cease, stop, or come to rest.
She welcomes it, teases him,
moves the dark gunnis of her close to him.

Rain soaks them as they contort.
They'll peel gum off trainer soles later
and curse the chewer who 'eaved it down.
Still they kiss, mollusc clamped.
The light still red, I smile, for I have known this.

The tamping bar of me is there,
the cobbing hammer inside beats,
the gads of my guts, prick and bleed.
The Cornish shovel skims, scatters and sighs.
The bob at Redruth still turns.

Bore a hole into me, whim,
that is charged with this passion,
a lode of love excavated right there
deep in life's mine
between Redruth railway station

(where men once traded all this
for cabins, lateens and costeens
on other pavements
[Steamship Passage to Quebec,
and Van Diemen's Land guaranteed].

Masses, from closed mines,
closed loves, closed kisses,
shut passion, knacked sex,
taking a chance for a better life,
from a sick that makes Cornwall tick)

and... the *Mining Exchange*,
the road to the *Radical Club*, *John Olivers*,
others to the *Druid's Hall*, the Penventon's nightclub
where once these two met,
and on an alcopop-fuelled whimsy, he asked her out.

Then, the lights go green,
as if I am brought to grass, flung into day.
In the mirror, in sunlight,
I see the girl frown. She has bruised lips
and he's no magazine.

The boy does not know of his elders,
who stood on the station,
but their anger, love, hate, fog
he knows well. Knacked, hurt, alone,
he's learnt how life turns, on another's whim.

Old Cornwall Society

First, the roll-call of the dead,
a minute's silence,
then the prayers for those unwell,
the news of who's gone in a home.

Next, the minutes of last month's meeting:
a precision account,
no debate needed.
Agreed. The chairman signs the book.

A small discussion: a coach or no
for the summer excursion?
A circular from the Grand Bard,
then the welcome to this evening's speaker.

The lights go out.
Slides and dialect, known places,
machinery debated. Mines. More mines.
Memories. Passion. Gathered fragments.

The stumbling words of thanks.
Hot taa, enforced biscuits.
"You'll have another wan't 'ee boy?
Some talk. You en't no ordinary fool."

The talk over, the old Cornish plod home,
after another night of returning choughs.
High on the hill, Nance watching,
like a big bezant.

Curse

If you are born Cornish
then the past always weighs heavy on you.

And the saddest thing in the world
is all those places I can go no longer,

where for some reason,
the past ways heavier there.

They were once happy,
but now they won't let me return.

They put up razor wire, searchlights,
barking Rottweilers to keep me out.

In any case, they are pasts
I should not return to, not ever.

Worse still though, is their closeness,
- they are stone's throws from me.

They are always, always, always there,
like a water torture of the mind.

There are faces there, I so do
and so don't want to see.

There are times there, I so don't
and so do want to see.

Yet all pasts turn on you.
They are selfish children.

They bite and savage the hand
that feeds and gives love.

Past pangs eat at me
like sugar rushes of time.

Unending memory.
It is the curse of my nation.

The Dodman Eastwards (For James Whetter)

That vexed, watery sky
(as if firmament and ocean
have forever swapped places)
washes over the Dodman's *Hack and Cast.*
I walk east, past an ochred Vault Beach,
the contorted farm at Lamledra,
on to Pen-a-mean's mackerel cliffs,
ancient lookout onto fields of fish.

The light changes at Gorran Haven
as on this November day, the sun slips.
It is *meez Due* as the Cornish has it:
'black month', and nights drawing in.
High on the still hill is Gorran Churchtown,
Anne Treneer's schoolhouse in the wind,
by the ghost of a *plen-an-gwarry*,
the road onto Heligan and St Ewe.

I hurry across the harbour, past cold gig rowers
and on the tight footpath by Trelispen.
You must have stood here James,
high over Penhaver's boulders,
by this Tumuli and haloed earthwork,
eye on the Gwineas, holy rocks,
mind on elections, votes, breakthrough.
Historian, politician, this is your coast.

I walk on, to the prow of Chapel Point,
arm of Portmellon, where shutters
hold back surf, sand and seaweed.
while bullocks piss steam into the turf.
If only we, with our way, words,
wishes, knowledge, books,
could leap as far as good Bodrugan,
then this night, all would be well.

Finds

I Rillaton Cup

Take a break down in Linkenhorne,
where they say, the devil was born.
Find there, this fairie cup of sheet gold,
corrugated like a field's furrow.
Dig down deep into Death's barrow
and spot a beaker below Bodmin's Moor.
Imagine then, a druidic potion,
    - held high in pagan devotion.

If George V, not knowing its significance
used it for his collar studs,
then surely, since I'm sleepy this morning,
    - a small Nescafé poured in, wouldn't hurt?

At moments like these, you find
you know yourself too well.
At the British Museum's Celtic section,
the discoveries aren't all on display.

Some are internal. They go back deep and long.
On your mind, they skip and play.
Dark secrets like barrows old.
Furrowed brows.
Finds inside.
Age brings no discoveries new and bold.
It just brushes away all that you know
    - all that you hold.

II Three Gold Lumulae

Material culture's moon-made gold,
stamped and scratched,
shaped to lie still, over skull and scapula;
these three are Kist kissed,
crescendic collars
of ceremony long ceased.

Finds from Harlyn Bay
and St. Juliot
now slung into cabinet,
for me and future me's
to gake at greatness.

Their metal is me,
more than just a mirror to ancient men.
Their blood, their sweat, their sperm, their piss
is all here, untouched by time or temporary burial.

Fluorescent tubes illumine the thin sheet,
as if just forged and fitted
on a summer's day.
I feel it upon my neck -
barrier, magic, talisman.

Thirty years gone and found.
If I'm lucky, then forty more.
What after four millennia will they find of me?
This poem? This place? These bones?
Enough. I'll be somewhere under stones.

Their metal is me.
If I believe that, I'm sure to be found.

III Trenoweth Collar

Hidden until 1793,
then yanked out, from tin-stream mud -
a boon on Brannel's Broadmoor.
You lay there for centuries
beneath blue-bell, peat and leaves,
a present for the future.

Nothing else - just this guilt jewel
of formalised pure palmettes
by branching comma motifs.
The leather is rotted where
each half joins the other, while
inlays shine for someone great.

I find in time's tart torque
all of us - risen from mud,
now thinking, jewelled objects
easily lost, split in two,
remote, unspeaking, and still,
at times bold brass, then cold zinc.

Like tin-streamer we stumble,
pan, swirl and gently wash,
looking for love's winsome find.
But tough torque, or flake of tin
- whatever treasure we win,
when the sun sets, the only find is dust.

Love and Seaweed

Tides.
Forever and ever,
come in tides.

You have seen them, felt their froth and their sweep.
They carry much: pebbles, mermaid's purses,
smoothed round glass, nets, shells, driftwood, love and lives.
Such tides are endless. They are cold. Bitter
as death, unforgiving and relentless.
They hold all that we do not wish to see.

Show me a man or woman who has not
felt the wreckage of love, of broken bows
smashed timbers, sunken hopes, joyless journeys.
All of us have voyaged on such vessels.
We know that they will run aground, but still
we unfold their sails, steer their tiller.
When it comes (we know it will always come),
that shipwreck is quick, fearful, terrible,
more terrible even than the desire
that once handed us the chart and compass.

We rise through the bubbles, through the deep waves
and wish then we had stayed safe on dry land,
never risking the curling green magic
of the hornpipe, heave and heart.

We swim between cold flotsam and jetsam,
pieces of us scattered through the world
at last coming to gather a small piece.
The piece found is not perfect at all
It is flawed, cracked, chipped, worn, but it will do.
'Es, most loves are like that.
Ours is not.
You washed in from the Gulf Stream at Newlyn,
where men know the true ocean, where each day,
they pit themselves against storm and seaweed,

gale and grey squall, for fish, shrimp, crab and life.
In Japan's waters you are named *nori*
Here you are *gubman*, *slatvara*, and *tang*,
Three in one - you are still the very same
whatever words, whatever the language.
When we two first bathed in the candlelight
your hair became seaweed, swaying, playing
yellow algae that brushed against my thigh.
It was the most beautiful thing I've seen.
From kelp to Celt, from Gulf Stream to Goonvean,
you are ocean and emotion, you are
my holdfast, my anchor in heavy surf.
You are love and seaweed, love and seaweed.

That energy, that seaweed has been there
since those first creatures, half-fish, half-frog
ambled out of that age's ancient soup
and gasped at the new air.
It wraps around
my feet now as a pair of bright green shoes.
And when St Michael the archangel came
he lived on nothing but this seaweed here
and the side-tossed tides and loving foam of
the Grey Rock that stands no more in the Wood.
Like him I first collected you in a basket
of willow, so the sea might fall away.
Even then, my polyp, I knew you'd come.
You would come in on the tide like Piran,
Ia and Meriasek, all of them.
They too, felt the weed at their tired feet,
swirling in real time with all the earth,
the rhythm of life, anthem of ages.
The saint's hands reach into the blue to gather.
Your hands there are seaweed too, my lover,
the way they wrap around me, entwine me.
Their clasp is wonderful, better, fuller
more natural than other promised lands.
I am lashed to them, a bond eternal.
The seagreenweed of you believes in me.
It goes beyond hair, eyes, face, lips and mind

but moves into me, swims and lifts me now.
I taste you miles from you and smell you
across far oceans, continents and space.
I shall feel you in death.
Yes, that too.
I shall hear you from beyond, sense it still.
Storms and Gales can blow right over us.
They are just shipping forecasts - just nothings.
Wind whips, seagulls rise, but we go under,
snuggle and relish the wet that's above,
the white waves that smash these cliffs where we walk.
Seaweed writes us, imagines our lives
floats in an aqua ink around this land,
a manuscript of our life and work,
knotwork illustrating our every move.
Seaweed fronds entwine beneath all of this.
These silent shapers heighten perception.

The cult of seaweed holds me in a trance.
On the shore, I worship its dance, your dance,
venerate its relics, its holiness.
You are that basal disk, that strong holdfast.
Coralloides and *Calcerum* deep below
watch us as we walk and talk this world.
They spy our splashing feet, our joy.
In but a moment, we can become them
breathing the tide, floating as if on air,
extracting all we can of this short life.
For certain, moments like this we have had.
They are everywhere, endless, joyous
like the sea itself.
One day I said that
I would not pick you up from the water,
since that - an unkind act - would dry you out,
You said that wouldn't matter.
It didn't.
When dried, hung up, you tell me the weather.
Aired, you become my forecast, my outlook.
Perhaps then you are to be eaten, consumed.
Weedgirl, I could stuff you in endlessly!
I crave salty tastes of ocean and rock.

Oh, I dream of this when we are asleep,
when your hair falls on my face in the night,
when occasionally a strand of it
catches in my mouth and I taste again
for real, all that I've dreamt and wished for.
It tightly binds me to you; you, to me.
That your hair is seaweed you d'know now.
It is the woven filaments of us.
I need the seaswash of you over me,
the terror and then thrill of submersion.
Compasses, charts, I've come to realise -
it's taken a lifetime on this heading
that I like the full feeling of drowning.

Other knowledge washes in alongside:
I can only live on peninsulas.
The truth is: I need the sea on three sides.
I need the air of the seaweed in me.
You are the same my seaweed woman,
raised on peninsulas, on Michigan,
on the jutting tailbone of Florida.
It is natural for you to be here.
When I cannot smell the seaweed or you,
I go mad, fall into oblivion,
when there are no seaweed chapels and wells,
no *bladderwrack* graves, quoits, menhirs and tombs,
when the seasway of the moors can't be heard,
when weed of shafts, adits, give no echo
when the *dulse* of my fogou is empty
and lost is the *wrack* of Hensbarrow.
When that's so, know my lover, my 'andsome,
that you'll always be my sushi wrapper,
the newly baked laverbread of my soul.
Your biology is mine. Mine is yours.
At symbiance we, locked to this grey rock.
Sleep or drowning can't ever tell me that.
Waters of weed though, still wash over me
turning the bluesky seagreen and I see
all those things which float between:
crabs, anemones, razor-shells, bone, blood,
detritus of this planet of water.

Well may you sneer those of you who were wrecked,
and found the imperfect love, that chipping
I have never had cause to hold or keep.
All of this that I say is true though,
truer than just cause, all that we fight for,
than that tongue, still spoken, and of that land
that wholly steers and guides our vessel.
Whatever we face, whatever parting,
I think only then of love and seaweed.
I hear your voice and I am enchanted.
The polyp of me is with you somewhere
in the ocean of life, distant yet still close.
Your colours maid, are still as beautiful.
They will always hold me, always, always.
Your slipperiness makes me smile now.
You are the true stem, true partner of life.

When we are long gone, we will still be there.
The fish may gnaw at us, tides will sweep us
but we shall float eternally my lover.
We shall be scattered, but we shall be strong.
Pieces will lie between the Dodman's Head
and Gerrans, on sands of Gugh and Agnes
many more between the Zawn and Zennor
Our small story shall be written there
etched in sea and rock for eternity.
When dead, the sea will wash over us both.

Resurrection follows. New polyps form.
Our seaweed floats again, unstoppable.
Sand eventually takes our place,
but we are the grains which will drift between
other seaweeds, to and from other loves,
we and they,
others,
all,
love and seaweed.